ANIMAL OPPOSITES

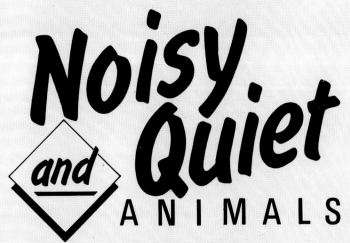

Mark Carwardine

Titles in this series
Daytime and Night-time Animals
Quick and Slow Animals
Big and Small Animals

First published in 1988 by
Wayland (Publishers) Ltd.
61 Western Road, Hove
East Sussex BN3 1JD
England

© Copyright 1988 Ilex Publishers Limited

British Library Cataloguing in Publication Data

Carwardine, Mark
 Noisy and quiet animals.—
 (Animal opposites).
 1. Animals—Juvenile literature
 I. Title II. Series
 591   QL49

ISBN 1-85210-298-5

Created and produced by
Ilex Publishers Ltd
29-31 George Street
Oxford OX1 2AJ

Designed by Paul Richards, Designers and Partners, Oxford

Illustrations by Martin Camm and Jim Channell
Bernard Thornton Artists

Printed in Spain by Gráficas Estella, S. A.

Cover illustration by Jim Channell
a chimpanzee and a python

Contents

Hyena	4
Shark	6
Howler monkey	8
Giant anteater	10
Indri	12
Python	14
Woodpecker	16
Mole	18
Wolf	20
Crocodile	22
Further information	24

The hyena is a noisy animal.

It makes strange giggles, yells, growls, howls and screams in the middle of the night.
This hyena is looking for a zebra or gazelle to eat.

The shark is a quiet animal.

It swims silently through the oceans in search of food. These sharks have needle-sharp teeth.

The howler monkey is a noisy animal.

It is the noisiest monkey in the world and its cries and howls can be heard from a long way away.
This howler monkey is hiding in a huge tree.

The giant anteater is a quiet animal.

It spends every day licking up thousands and thousands of ants.
This anteater has found an ants' nest.

The indri is a noisy animal.

It makes the loudest noise of any animal in Madagascar.
This indri is leaping from one tree to another.

The python is a quiet animal.

It rarely makes a sound as it slides along in search of food.
This python is coiled around a branch.

The woodpecker is a noisy animal.

It makes a tremendous din as it pecks and drums on tree trunks.
This woodpecker is pecking out a hole in which to lay its eggs.

The mole is a quiet animal.

It spends most of its life hiding underground.
This mole is digging a new tunnel.

The wolf is a noisy animal.

Its 'lonesome howl' can be heard for miles around. This wolf is howling to other members of its pack.

The crocodile is a quiet animal.

It makes so little noise – and lies so still – that it is often mistaken for a log.
This crocodile is sunbathing on the edge of a riverbank.

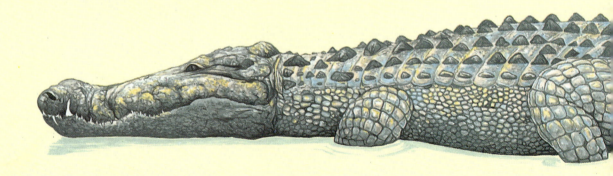

Further information

Crocodile *page 22*. Crocodiles are well camouflaged; they wait quietly along the edge of rivers, ready to attack unsuspecting animals, such as deer and monkeys, when they come down to the water's edge to drink.

Giant anteater *page 10*. The giant anteater must eat more than 20,000 ants each day to survive; it uses its 60-centimetre-long tongue to flick up more than 200 ants every minute.

Howler monkey *page 8*. The howler monkey's call sounds rather like a lion's roar; this helps to keep other howler monkeys, in neighbouring groups, away from its favourite trees.

Hyena *page 4*. Hyenas occur in many parts of Africa and Asia; they will eat almost anything, including skin, hair, bones, horns and hooves.

Indri *page 12*. The indri is a very rare animal, found only in a few jungles on the slopes of volcanoes in Madagascar; it belongs to a group of animals known as the lemurs.

Mole *page 18*. Moles live in many parts of Europe, North America, Asia and Africa; they are well adapted for digging, with powerful front feet which are shaped like shovels.

Python *page 14*. The python belongs to a group of snakes known as the constrictors; it is not poisonous but kills its prey by coiling around it and squeezing.

Shark *page 6*. The shark is a fish; not all sharks are dangerous to people – some of the biggest eat tiny marine animals called plankton.

Wolf *page 20*. Wolves keep in touch by howling, which may be used to call the pack together after a hunt or to warn neighbouring packs to stay away.

Woodpecker *page 16*. Woodpeckers drum against tree trunks for many different reasons; they drum to declare themselves the owners of a territory, to search for grubs under the bark and to hollow out their nesting holes.